SIMPLY VB.NET

Never a dull moment

Richard Thomas Edwards

CONTENTS

Introduction

Chapter Subtitle

When I started working on this book, I realized that putting something like this wasn't for me to just hash back through what I know about VB.NET or convince you that VB.NET is something you should learn.

Instead, what I needed to be doing is helping you learn VB.NET.

But how can you teach a language like VB.NET without sounding like an English teacher? After all, you do have words and concepts similar to teaching English which must be taught so that a sentence makes sense.

Furthermore, since I'm no longer working for Microsoft and I am certainly not an English professor, other than my passion for writing and sharing my wealth of information with you, why would you want to read what I have to say anyway?

Never-the-less, here I am presenting to you a book on learning VB.NET and I'm hoping, if you're are still reading this, that you will find this book helpful.

Also, you better have a good sense of humor. Because, every once in a while I even surprise myself with some hum dingers.

Wait, you can't drop out of this e-book!

How can you drop out of a class if you am not in one, right?

My first experience of a student wanting to drop out of a college class was based on a heated conversation between the professor and the student. I'm not quite certain why the student felt the way she did considering the professor was an excellent, well known poet.

But for some reason only known to her, she didn't take much liking to him and she wasn't in his class past that point.

Which brings me to my real point that I want to make in your behalf. I don't have to be liked by you. Nor do you have to return the favor. The bottom line here is you are investing the use of your time, effort and money into this book because it is going to gratify your interest of wanting to learn a programming language.

One that, in return is going to make you look smarter on paper, increase your wages and otherwise help you become the superman or superwoman.

Well, I can't promise that. At least, not all of that.

You are paying me to share with you my 30 years-worth of time in front of a computer screen in hopes some of that genie stuff will wear off on you. I can't promise that either. Yes, I am well familiar with the fact that this is the chapter where you decide to purchase this e-book. But, I don't want to motivate you if you're just looking for page after page of code.

You can get that from the internet for free. Instead, I'm taking a more relaxed approach and hope you will appreciate the fact that I know learning a computer language is more than knowing what is needed to code with it. You have to sell yourself and your skills to others. After all, if you can't do that, I don't care how popular the language here is in helping you land a job, not helping you own the right to respectful wages is more important.

Otherwise, nothing changes in your life no matter how passionate you are about becoming a freelance programmer or IT consultant. Still want to close the introduction to this book and walk away?

Great!

I don't have to worry about you being my competition the next time I go in for an interview.

I'm currently running Visual Studio 2010. But there is a version that you can download called Visual studio 2017 Community which is free.

First, I'm not going to help you install Visual Basic. Simply click on this link and download the installer. From there, the installer will guide you through the process of getting it installed.

When you have this up, come back – after you have a new blank VB windows project up – I'll take it from there.

You are now ready to start programming with Visual Basic

The Green Diamond

Just below Test and Analyze is this immediately followed by the word start. Please click that now.

You should see this:

Pretty boring stuff, right?

Nothing happened other than a blank form was displayed. Click on the red rectangle on the running form and close it. Now, go over to the right where it says properties, look for the word Text and change the form name to Window 1. Run it again and that name will appear on it as it also appears on the design form.

Close the running form.

Over on the left side will be the word toolbox click on it and it will expand out. There will be a menu option there for All Windows Forms and if you expand that, you will find the word button to the right of an icon that looks like one.

If you double click on it, and then move your cursor away from the Toolbox Menu so that it closes, you will find a button has been placed on the form.

Should look something like this:

When a control is highlighted – done by simply clicking on it – an adjustment border will surround the control.

Also, the properties for that control will be displayed on the right. Look for the Button's Text property and change it to Click Me!

Run the form.

You can click on the button again and again. It will give you the same result.

Nothing happens.

Yes, I know how disturbing it is to have to do this? But there is a point to be made here:

Nothing will happen!

Why?

Because event driven code does nothing without code either getting the job you want to do under that button or conforming that you clicked it.

Since there is no code under it, you get no gratitude from the program because it is doing nothing.

You have to have write code to perform tasks and show your users why you put that button on the form for a reason.

If your response to your users was you wanted to drive them crazy, good job!

But if you want a job as a programmer, double click on the button and add this line:

```
Public Class Form1

    Private Sub Button1_Click(sender As Object, e As EventArgs) Handles Button1.Click

        Messagebox.show("Sorry, that didn't help much but thanks for playing.")
```

```
        End Sub

End Class
```

A bit of House humor.

This is what happens after you click the button:

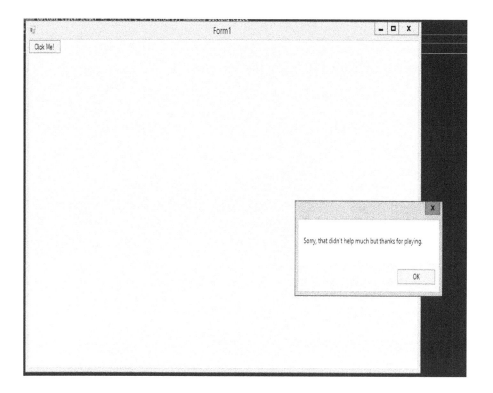

Since I'm -- and I am sure you are -- already getting extremely bored with the basics of a modified "Hello World", let me ask, do you have Excel installed?

If you do, great. If you don't, just sit back and watch. I'm about to show you your first bug.

Anyone who has worked with Object Oriented Programming knows that objects are not shared between events.

Instead of the MessageBox.Show line, replace it with this:

```
Dim oExcel as Object = CreateObject("Excel.Appliction")
```

So, if you create an Excel.Application, for example inside a button click event, you should never actually see the Application show up. Perhaps, a flicker of it.

BUG ALERT

Well, it showed up in all its glory. As shown below. And that is not supposed to happen.

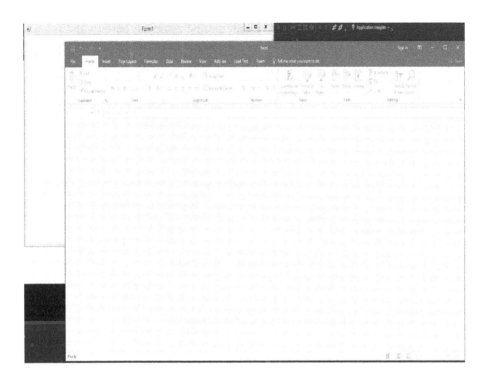

And to also prove that each event doesn't see the other, I added another Button and tried to type in the code I want to use to close it:

```
Private Sub Button1_Click(sender As Object, e As EventArgs) Handles Button1.Click
    Dim oExcel As Object = CreateObject("Excel.Application")
    oExcel.Visible = True
End Sub

Private Sub Button2_Click(sender As Object, e As EventArgs) Handles Button2.Click
    oExcel.Close
    oExcel = Nothing
End Sub
```

Those red wavy lines are basically telling me I'm stupid for trying.

How do I get around this?

TIP: If you want persistence and have the ability to work with an object such as Excel throughout your project, place its null or nothing reference right after the Public Class declaration at the top of your form, class or module.

I take the reference to the Excel object and put it above the two events and outside of any other events as seen below:

```vb
Public Class Form1
    Dim oExcel As Object = Nothing
    Private Sub Button1_Click(sender As Object, e As EventArgs) Handles Button1.Click
        oExcel = CreateObject("Excel.Application")
        oExcel.Visible = True
    End Sub

    Private Sub Button2_Click(sender As Object, e As EventArgs) Handles Button2.Click

        If IsNothing(oExcel) = False Then
            oExcel.Close
            oExcel = Nothing
        End If

    End Sub
End Class
```

Notice that I also added a conditional loop which tests the validity of the existence of the Excel object.

Okay so here's the two up:

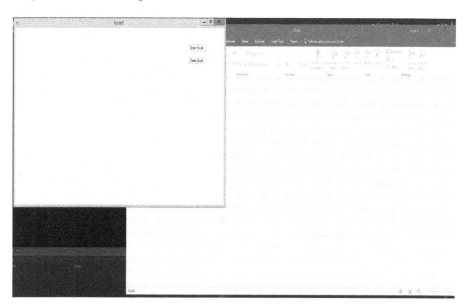

After clicking the close button:

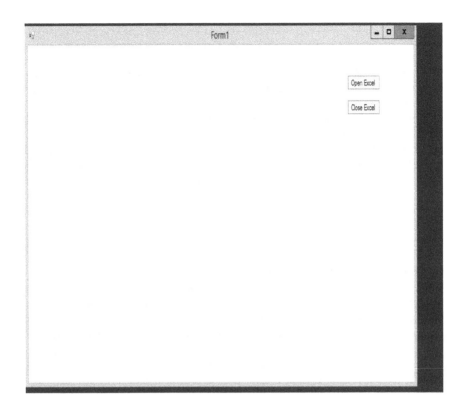

And I'm left with a form that while functional, really doesn't do anything for my unemployment status.

But I do want to show you one more thing – it gets asked in interviews.

What happens to routines such as the buttons we've created code for when you remove the buttons from the form?

The answer, the designer removes the event handlers

Let's give them something to talk about

There's a song with the same a similar line and it made millions. Doubt that I using the same will have a similar effect on my life. I'm also at the other end of the life cycle spectrum. And I can tell you right now, the times that I got hired for a job in IT, was because I gave them a story that went like this:

Before you met me, you didn't realize how much value and important I am to you and your team's desire to accomplishing the task at hand. Now that you've met me, you know I am the asyou were looking for and have no choice but to hire me on the spot.

The name of the game here is **the art of selling**. One I pretty much wrote back in the '80s.

Right now, lets start with a humble beginning

Yes, I play Drakes Uncharted. No, I don't like the fact that Drake isn't going into Uncharted 5.

Start VB.NET. Create a standard project and add a Module to it. We're going to use this project for all the work we're planning on doing in VB.NET for two reasons.

One, All the routines can be called from the form load.

Two, the examples that we are doing in this will show you just how easy it is to build a ton of cool stuff rather quickly.

In the module Type:
Public Sub Create_A_MessageBox(ByVal msg As String)
   Call MsgBox(msg)
End Sub

Now, go to the form
   Private Sub Form1_Load(ByVal sender As System.Object, ByVal e As System.EventArgs) Handles MyBase.Load

   Module1.Create_A_MessageBox ("This is a message box")
End Sub

Run the project. This is what you should see:

Input Box

Public Sub Create_An_InputBox(ByVal msg As String)
   Dim answer
   answer = InputBox(msg)
End Sub

Now, go to the form
   Private Sub Form1_Load(ByVal sender As System.Object, ByVal e As System.EventArgs) Handles MyBase.Load

   Module1.Create_An_InputBox ("This is a input box")
End Sub

Run it.

Here's what you'll see:

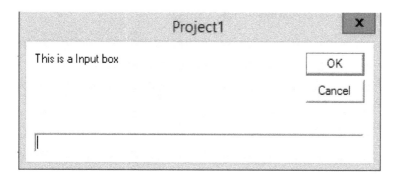

```
Public Sub Create_A_Popup(ByVal msg As String)
    Dim ws as Object
    we = CreateObject("WScript.Shell")
    Call ws.Popup(msg)
End Sub
```

Now, go to the form

```
Private Sub Form1_Load(ByVal sender As System.Object, ByVal e As System.EventArgs) Handles MyBase.Load

    Module1.Create_A_Popup("This is a popup")
End Sub
```

Run it

Here's what you'll see:

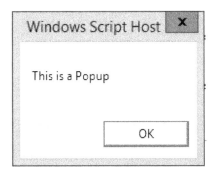

.NET MESSAGEBOX

```
Public Sub Create_Message_BOX(ByVal Message As String)

    MessageBox.Show(Message)

End Sub
```

```
Private Sub Form1_Load(ByVal sender As System.Object, ByVal e As System.EventArgs) Handles MyBase.Load

    Module1.Create_Message_BOX(".Net MessageBox")

End Sub
```

WHAT TIME IS IT

```
Public Sub What_Time_Is_It()
  Dim t As String
  t = Format$(Now, "hh:mm:ss AM/PM")
  Call MsgBox(t)
End Sub
```

Now, go to the form

```
Private Sub Form1_Load(ByVal sender As System.Object, ByVal e As System.EventArgs) Handles MyBase.Load
```

```
    Module1.What_Time_Is_It ()
End Sub
```

Run it.

Here's What You'll see:

```
Public Sub What_Day_Is_It()
    Dim d As String
    d = Format$(Now, "MM/DD/YYYY")
    Call MsgBox(d)
End Sub
```

Now, go to the form

```
Private Sub Form1_Load(ByVal sender As System.Object, ByVal e As System.EventArgs) Handles MyBase.Load


    Module1.What_Day_Is_It()
End Sub
```

Run it.
Here's what you will see:

I think we're off to a great start. Everyone of these can be manipulated. We even manipulated the date and time with the Format$ function.

NOT ANOTHER HELLO WORLD!

Yes, it is time for that infamous moment when you experience the distinct pleasure of creating a dumb, but important beginning of your VB.NET trek. Oh, wait a minute, didn't you already do that? Yes, you did, in spades.

Now, go to the form and type in, again, the module1 code below.

```
Private Sub Form1_Load(ByVal sender As System.Object, ByVal e As System.EventArgs) Handles MyBase.Load


    Module1.Create_A_MessageBox ("Hello World")
End Sub
```

Run the project. This is what you should see:

Let's Start having some real fun!

VB.Net Forms

As you already have seen, VB.Net forms are different. They are also easier to use.

The mdi form

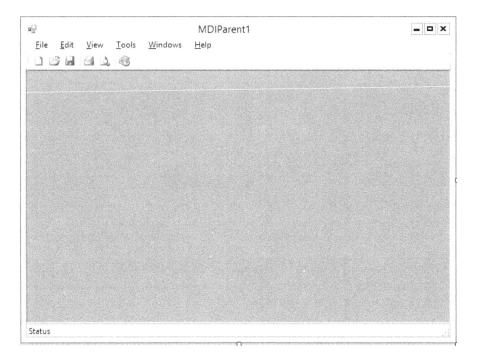

If there is any one form that gets used quite often, it his this one. Not only is there some useful code in the code window for you to learn from, this form is also a parent form which enables you to work with more than one form. What we call parent child form.

While adding one to your project is a good move, you still need to perform an additional step and make it the startup form. That is done by going to the solution explorer and double clicking on my project.

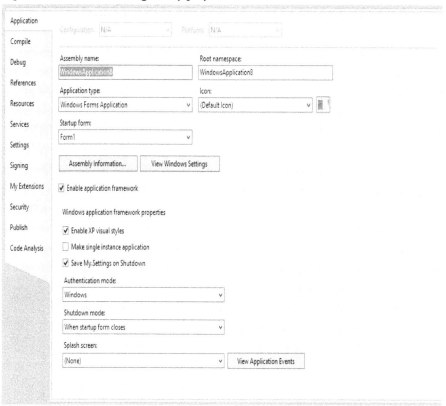

See where it says Startup form? By default, it is for Form1. it to MDIParent1 and then run the project.

Once the form is running, go to the MDIParent1 menu and to File. Click it and then click New. Do the same thing again. What you should be seeing is two forms inside the MDIParent1 form and two child forms.

Here's what the form should look like:

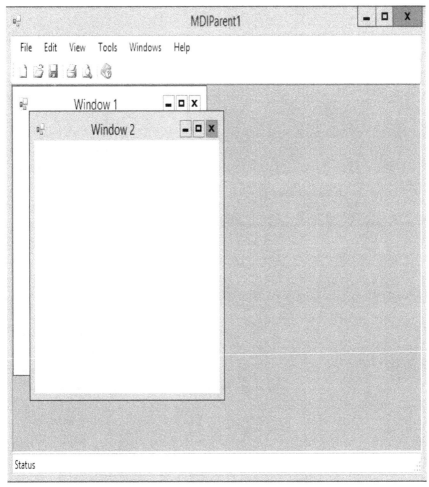

Okay, close the MDIParent1. And switch back to the Form1 as the startup form.

Tip

No matter what language you are using for your code, once you build a form in Visual Studio, the form you build can be used by that language.

Entering your First Name, Middile Initial and Last name.

Please do the following:

Add three labels and caption them:

Label1.Text: First Name

Label2.Text: MI

Label3.Text: Last Name

Add three text controls and place them under each one of the labels.

Textbox1 under Label1

Textbox2 under Label2

Textbox3 under Label3

Make Textbox2 small enough so that one letter can be entered and the maxlength property from 0 to 1.

Add two Command buttons to the right of the labels and text. It should look something like this:

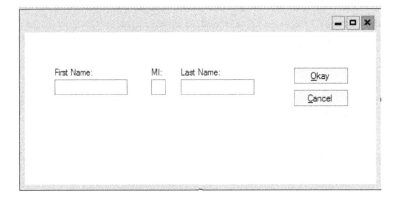

Now, add the code below:

Private Sub Command1_Click()

```
Public Class Form1

    Private Sub Form1_Load(ByVal sender As System.Object, ByVal e As System.EventArgs) Handles MyBase.Load

    End Sub

    Private Sub Button1_Click(ByVal sender As System.Object, ByVal e As System.EventArgs) Handles Button1.Click

        If TextBox1.Text = "" Then
            MsgBox("Please enter a First Name before clicking here.")
            Exit Sub
        End If

        If TextBox2.Text = "" Then
            MsgBox("Please enter a Middle Initial before clicking here.")
            Exit Sub
        End If

        If TextBox3.Text = "" Then
            MsgBox("Please enter a Last Name before clicking here.")
```

```
        Exit Sub

    End If



    Call MsgBox("Hello " & TextBox1.Text & " " & TextBox2.Text & " " & TextBox3.Text, , "Thank You")



    End Sub



    Private Sub Button2_Click(ByVal sender As System.Object, ByVal e As System.EventArgs) Handles
Button2.Click

        Me.Close()

    End Sub
```

As expected, you fail to add anything requested of you, a msgbox comes up and lets you know about it and when they are filled, you get this:

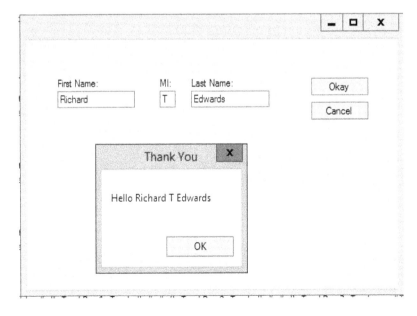

Now, I like adding more information so it looks as though I'm giving them a little extra for their time. You could add the following:

Module1. What_Day_Is_It()

Module1. What_Time_Is_It()

But that just makes them have to click buttons. The next alternative is to add these to the original message box. But that looks pretty ugly too. So, I decided to do this:

```
Private Sub Button1_Click(ByVal sender As System.Object, ByVal e As System.EventArgs) Handles Button1.Click

    If TextBox1.Text = "" Then

        MsgBox("Please enter a First Name before clicking here.")

        Exit Sub

    End If


    If TextBox2.Text = "" Then

        MsgBox("Please enter a Middle Initial before clicking here.")

        Exit Sub

    End If


    If TextBox3.Text = "" Then

        MsgBox("Please enter a Last Name before clicking here.")

        Exit Sub

    End If



    Dim tstr As String
```

```
    tstr = "Hello " & TextBox1.Text & " " & TextBox2.Text & " " & TextBox3.Text & vbCrLf

    tstr = tstr & "The current time is: " & TimeOfDay.ToLongTimeString & vbCrLf

    tstr = tstr & "The current Date is: " & Date.Today & vbCrLf

    MsgBox(tstr, , "Thank You")

  End Sub



  Private Sub Button2_Click(ByVal sender As System.Object, ByVal e As System.EventArgs) Handles
Button2.Click

    Me.Close()

  End Sub
```

And it looks like this:

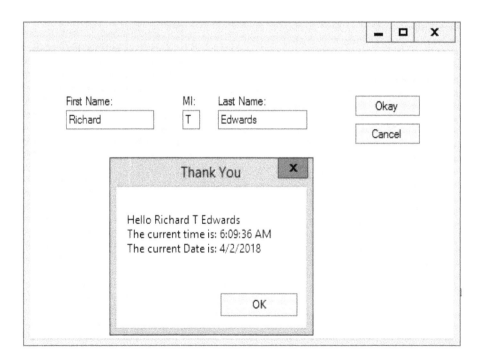

I like that and I think the user will too.

Make the user do what we want or quit the program

Which is exactly what we just did – well almost. The effect is known as bullet proofing and the idea is simple, give the user no opportunity to provide wrong information. Well, as short as this e-book, just keep it simple.

```
If TextBox1.Text = "" Then

    MsgBox("Please enter a First Name before clicking here.")

    Exit Sub

End If


If TextBox2.Text = "" Then

    MsgBox("Please enter a Middle Initial before clicking here.")

    Exit Sub

End If


If TextBox3.Text = "" Then

    MsgBox("Please enter a Last Name before clicking here.")

    Exit Sub

End If
```

That's about as simple as one can get to assure the user is putting something in each text but no where near good enough bullet proofing. And by the way, these simple routines at this level of testing would be what is called functionality testing.

Working with the notion of binding

In the world of VB – and I mean VB3, VB4, VB5, VB6 and VB.Net – there is this concept known as Binding. You can have early Binding, Mixed Binding and Late Binding.

The reason for this is quite simple, you to make a reference to a type library in VB:

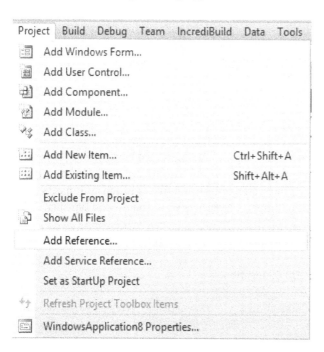

When this is clicked, another menu comes up. I've purposely chose the COM tab because this book is based on using COM – Component Object Model – references in this book. So the image looks like this:

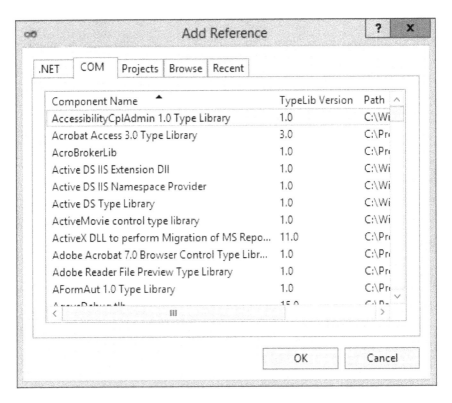

Do down the list until you Microsoft ActiveX Data Objects 6.0 Library. I've purposely selected this because I plan on using it to show you the differences in binding. Once selected, click OK. You have one more step to take and that is to add an Imports statement to the top of the form. Imports ADODB is what you need to type just above the Public Class Form1.

After you've make a reference, you can choose to do the following:

Early Binding:

Dim Cn as Object As New ADODB.Connection

Or:

Dim Cn as Object As ADODB.Connection

cn = New ADODB.Connection

Mixed Binding:
Dim Cn as Object As ADODB.Connection
cn = CreateObject("ADODB.Connection")

Late Binding:
Dim Cn as Object
cn = CreateObject("ADODB.Connection")

Late binding uses no reference to a Type Library making it harder to code but less likely to have version issues.
Mixed binding uses a reference to a Type Library but usually only to make it much easier to code.
Once the coding is done, the code can either be run as is or be quickly converted to late binding.
Early binding is done for the explicit purpose of knowing ever user will have the same type library available for the program so that it works exactly the way the program is supposed to work on every other machine.
Which is why I have chosen to write all the code in this e-book using late binding. No dll hell here!.

Working with Internet Explorer

There are a couple of ways you can run explorer from your desktop.
One, you can create a shortcut like the way you have been doing. But you still have to type in the web page once it is up.
Two, you can use Wscript. Shell and use the run function:

```
Public Sub Create_IE()

Dim ws as Object

ws = CreateObject("WScript.Shell")
ws.Run ("HTTPS://www.Google.com")


End Sub

Public Sub Create_IE_2()


Dim ie as Object

ie = CreateObject("InternetExplorer.Application")
ie.Visible = True
ie.Navigate2 ("https://www.yahoo.com")


End Sub
```

Three, you can use InternetExplorer.Application class and create an instance of IE that way.

While these do work, to create an instance of IE, there are some issues with each that does make it hard for you to know when the object you created in code has ended. Why would that even concern you, right?
It probably shouldn't. After all, the whole objective here is to start an instance if IE and tell it where you want to go.
   But what if you needed to know exactly when the instance you created either stopped running or was shut down by the person using it?
As it turns out, VB.NET doesn't have a direct way to know when processes start and when they end. The script simply gets IE started and, well, is finished working after that point. It is known as the process going out of scope.
But what if you could? Below is one way of doing it.

```
Public Sub Create_IE_3()

Dim ie as Object
Dim ws as Object
Dim fso

ie = CreateObject("InternetExplorer.Application")
ie.Visible = True
ie.Navigate2 ("https://www.yahoo.com")
MsgBox ("Running.")
Do While ie = "Internet Explorer"
   WScript.Sleep (250)
Loop
MsgBox ("Explorer stopped running.")
End Sub
```

Did it work?
What you should see happen, is the ie code worked just fine. It isn't until I try being smart that loop that I get in trouble. Why? Simple, we're wanting to make sure that when ie is no longer around, I get notified. The problem is, the darn thing turns into a null!
So, I get an error.

Wow! Imagine my surprise!

Okay, so let's give it some snake oil charm!

```
Public Sub Create_IE_43()

Dim ie as Object
Dim ws as Object

ie = CreateObject("InternetExplorer.Application")
ie.Visible = True
ie.Navigate2 ("https://www.yahoo.com")
MsgBox ("Running.")

On Error Resume Next
Do While ie = "Internet Explorer"
  If Err.Number <> 0 Then
    Err.Clear
    Exit Sub
  End If
  WScript.Sleep (250)
Loop
MsgBox ("Explorer stopped running.")

End Sub
```

This is sincerely, some dangerous code. Not because it actually works but because it shouldn't work, it does work but for all the wrong reasons. In fact, if you were to remove the On Error Resume next, the code would error as it normally does.
Please consider why that could turn out to be a big deal. You are supposed to get errors and those errors should not be ignored.
In this particular case, the loop that I are using is no longer being challenged for making sure it stops looping through the sleep cycle when IE <> "Internet Explorer."
What I are saying to it with the On Error Resume next is that while IE doesn't return "Internet Explorer", I don't care what happens if it errors, I just want to continue running no matter what happens.
Which would be fine if IE was returning a string value that no longer said "Internet Explorer" but it doesn't and since it is not a string value that can be evaluated as a string, an error occurs and continues to occur every time the loop tries to evaluate

the value. And using On Error Resume Next, you've basically told the loop to run forever. The only thing between you and the other side of the employment door is this:

```
If err.Number <> 0 then
    err.clear
    Exit Do
End If
```

The first time you bring a server down because your code didn't trap for errors in a loop and it runs out of memory or that computer's performance takes a hit because of it is when you're out the door. This is a much better way to handle it.

Please add a class –use the default – and then add a reference to the Microsoft WMI Scripting V1.2 Library.
Copy and paste the code below into the empty class code window. Also, watch out for the quotes in this book. You're going to want to replace all of them in the VB environment.

```
Public WithEvents sink As SWbemSink
Dim ProcessId As Integer
Dim v As Integer

Private Sub sink_OnObjectReady(ByVal objWbemObject As
WbemScripting.ISWbemObject, ByVal objWbemAsyncContext As
WbemScripting.ISWbemNamedValueSet)

Select Case objWbemObject.Path_.Class

    Case "___InstanceCreationEvent"

      obj = objWbemObject.Properties_.Item("TargetInstance").Value
      If obj.Properties_.Item("Name").Value = "iexplore.exe" Then
        If ProcessId = 0 Then
          ProcessId = obj.Properties_.Item("ProcessId").Value
          MsgBox ("Process has Started.")
        End If
      End If
```

```vb
    Case "__InstanceDeletionEvent"

        obj = objWbemObject.Properties_.Item("TargetInstance").Value
        If ProcessId = obj.Properties_.Item("ProcessId").Value Then
          MsgBox ("Process has ended.")
        v = 1
        End If

    End Select

End Sub

Public Sub Start_Monitoring()
v = 0
svc = GetObject("Winmgmts:\\.\root\cimv2")
svc.Security_.AuthenticationLevel = 6
svc.Security_.ImpersonationLevel = 3
sink = CreateObject("WbemScripting.SWbemSink")
Call svc.ExecNotificationQueryAsync(sink, "SELECT * FROM
__InstanceOperationEvent WITHIN 1 WHERE TargetInstance ISA 'Win32_Process'
and TargetInstance.Name = 'iexplore.exe'")

Dim ie As Object

ie = CreateObject("InternetExplorer.Application")
ie.Visible = True
ie.Navigate2 ("https://www.Google.com")

Do While v = 0
  DoEvents
Loop

End Sub
```

And the Form:
```vb
Private Sub Form_Load()
        Dim MyClass As New Class1
        MyClass.Start_Monitoring
End Sub
```

So now, we have a class that when created monitors when IE gets started and then waits for the processId of the instance of iexplorer to close.

When the program runs, it waits for ie to get started and is alerted to that fact.

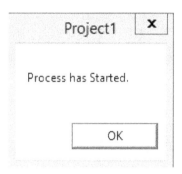

That processId is kept until the process shuts down and then, when told the process was deleted it let's you know about it.

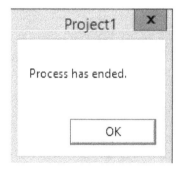

Well that keep on going will without some error trapping:

If err.Number <> 0 then
    err.clear
    Exit do
  End If

Without it, the program would never get out of the loop. Hence the reason why I call it snake oil charm. Bear that in mind when you start using error trapping because it is out to bite you in the butt if you're not careful!

Okay, let's have smore fun.

NEVER BROKEN OUT OF THE BOX

I can't tell you how many times I heard that from my fellow workers at Microsoft Technical Support. Yes, in some cases, a lot of that is true but in more often than not a Quick Fix Engineering Went through the pipeline to fix an issue that wasn't resolved before shipping the product.

Sometimes, it is really broken out of the box.

Okay, so here's a couple of things we should talk about first before moving on.

Never cut and paste code from here

I'm trying to cover a lot of the same turf with the same concepts and not all languages support the Garamond quotes. It is a good idea to replace the quotes with regular straight quotes and not the fancy ones that are used in this text.

PERSISTANCE

VB.NET is an event driven language As such what is in an event stays with the event. Try this:

Create a new project and add a button to a form. This assumes you have 32 bit office installed. Double click on the form and add:

Dim oExcel as Object

oExcel = CreateObject("Excel.Application")

oExcel.Visible = true

Then run the project and click the button. For a split second you will see Excel and come up and go away.

TIP: If you want persistence and have the ability to work with an object such as Excel throughout your project, place its null or nothing reference right after the Public Class declaration at the top of your form, class or module.

I take the reference to the Excel object and put it above the two events and outside of any other events as seen below:

Dim oExcel as Object

```
Private Sub Button1_Click(ByVal sender As System.Object, ByVal e As System.EventArgs) Handles Button1.Click
```

oExcel = CreateObject("Excel.Application")

oExcel.Visible = true

```
End Sub
```

```
        Private Sub Button2_Click(ByVal sender As System.Object, ByVal e As System.EventArgs) Handles
Button2.Click

        Try

                oExcel.Quit()

                oExcel = nothing

        Catch ex As Exception



        End Try

End Sub
```

I use try catch because when an error does occur, I don't have to apologize for the program exiting abruptly.

The 12 Essential COM Coding pieces to the COM Kingdom

There are 12 lines of code types used today in every language. These are:

1. The creation of an object
2. The use of a property to get\a value
3. The use of a function that does or does not accept parameters and may or may not return a value. Functions are also called methods.
4. The use of an event that occurs and you write code to respond to it.
5. The use of enumerators
6. The use of conditional Loops
7. The use of conditional branches
8. The use of error trapping
9. Data Conversions
10. Constants
11. Declarations
12. Reg Expressions

CREATION OF THE OBJECT

Every language that works with Windows and Office products has a way to communicate with them. In VB.NET, this is done two ways.
The words here that are used are CreateObject and GetObject.

CREATEOBJECT

So, what is CreateObject? The sugar coated answer is that it creates something that can be used to perform a task. In-other-words, if Office is installed, and you typed:

oWord = CreateObject("Word.Application")

Once, you've created the object, you have a way to communicate with it.

oWord.Visible = true

CreateObject was modified back around 2000 to include the ability to connect to a remote machine. With all the security and firewalls in place, it is doubtful that would be worth trying today.

GETOBJECT

GetObject is old school. Used to be a time when you could use it for a lot of different things. It works like CreateObject in that you can create an object but is primarily used today with Winmgmts and WinNT.

svc = GetObject("winmgmts:\\.\root\cimv2")

Again, once you've created the object, you can use the object reference.

svc.Security_.AuthenticationLevel =6

Please don't try these. They are examples that do work. You'll be able to see them in action much later. There is a lot more to in order to make the above code segments worth your while using.

Besides, creating objects is the fun and easy part of this truly fascinating journey. And like any puzzle, every part that will be covered here is one step closer to completing it.

The use of a property to get\a value

Properties can be something that you create or something that has already been created for you.

If for example, you decided that a property needed to be like shown in the above example to 6:

svc.Security_.AuthenticationLevel =6

Okay, so how do you find out what the property was before I changed it?

Dim old

old = svc.Security_.AuthenticationLevel

Yes, it is just that simple.

What if you wanted to create your own property?

First dimension it:

Dim myproperty

Next it:

myproperty = 25

Next, get it:

Dim old

49

old = myproperty

Okay, so why would you want to a property to 25 knowing getting the property would return 25? Well, there are situations where a return value would tell you whether or not something returned with an return value that was greater than zero and if checked, whether or not the call worked

Dim iret

iret = 0

iret = ws.Run("Notepad.exe")

METHODS TO FUNCTION OR TO SUB THAT IS THE QUESTION

What is a method?

A method is a sub or function that can be created by the program to perform a task or called by your program to perform a task that the calling program knows is available and knows how to use it.

Technically, the creation of an object falls under the category of a method as it is a function that returns a value. It is only highlighted a key to the kingdom because of its importance to writing a program.

It is also a way in which zero or more properties can be passed in. These can be for private or public and they can be a function or a sub.

Function examples:

Function GetValue(ByVal Name As String , ByVal obj As String)
End Function

Private Function GetValue(ByVal Name As String , ByVal obj As String)
End Function

Public Function GetValue(ByVal Name As String , ByVal obj As String)
End Function

Sub examples:

Sub SetValue(ByVal Name As String , ByVal obj As String, ByVal Name As String , ByVal obj As String)
End Sub

Private Sub SetValue(ByVal Name As String , ByVal obj As String)
End Sub

Public Sub SetValue(ByVal Name As String , ByVal obj As String)

End Sub

When calling a sub or function, unless it is specified as being an optional value, all properties must be satisfied otherwise, the function or sub will either not work or raise an error.

For example, when the below code is called in this manner, it still works:

```
locator = CreateObject("WbemScripting.SWbemLocator")
```

```
svc = locator.ConnectServer()
```

Despite the fact that there are 8 variables that can be passed in:

```
svc = locator.ConnectServer(".",  "root\cimV2", Username, Password, Locale,
Authority, Security Flags, SWbemNamedValueSet)
```

The reason for these properties being setup this way was simple, unless you are trying to connect to a remote machine, UserName and Password would cause an error. Unless you are going to the default namespace: root\cimV2; and planning on using one of the classes: Win32_LogicalDisk, for example, if the class you are wanting to use is located elsewhere other than the default, you have to specify it before you attempt to use that class.

events YOU CAN respond to it

Windows in an event driven environment and as such, your VB.NET program can create event routines which tell you something has happened and you can respond to it. Here's an example of an event you can create in code that was created in VB.NET that works:

```
Dim w
w = 0
Private Sub sink_OnObjectReady(ByVal objWbemObject, ByVal
objWbemAsyncContext)
    For Each prop In objWbemObject.Properties_
      v = v + prop.Name & " " & GetValue(prop.Name, objWbemObject) & vbCrLf
    Next
    MsgBox (v)
End Sub
```

This is called an Async Event call because the program can perform other tasks while waiting for this event to fire off asynchronously.

The problem is, scripts don't just sit around waiting for events to happen isn't what the script likes to do. It likes to do what it needs to perform the task at hand and exit. And that's where I use a bit of VB.NET magic.

```
Do While w = 0
  WScript.Sleep(500)
Loop
```

When the Async call, in this case, is completed, the controller of the event raises an event called OnCompleted:

```
Private Sub sink_OnCompleted(ByVal iHResult, ByVal objWbemErrorObject, ByVal objWbemAsyncContext)
  w = 1
End Sub
```

And when this happens the loop that keeps the script running, reads the change in W and knows a w=1 means it is done and the code moves on to do whatever else is left to do.

Also, in some cases Async calls don't need an event function to happen.

Here's another example:

```
es = Svc.ExecNotificationQuery("Select * From ___InstanceCreationEvent WITHIN 1 where TargetInstance ISA 'Win32_Process'")

Do While w < 5
  ti = es.NextEvent(-1)
  obj = ti.Properties_.Item("TargetInstance").Value
    For Each prop In objWbemObject.Properties_
      v = v + prop.Name & " " & GetValue(prop.Name, obj) & vbCrLf
    Next
    MsgBox (v)
    w=w+1
Loop
```

This may appear as though it is not asynchronous, but if you consider the pattern, you can see that the notification isn't just doing it once, it is doing it 4 times and is responding to the event as it happens. And not because you want it to happen 4 times.

Technically speaking there are two of these that VB.NET uses. For Each and For

For Each obj in objs

Next

For x=0 To rs.Fields.Count-1

Next

These are technically non-conditional enumerators because they are not based on a conditional which must be proven to be true of false.

For Each is based on a enumerating through as collection of objects. You will be seeing a lot of this kind of enumerator when I work with WBemScripting because the objects collection and the properties collection are a natural fit for this kind of information processing.

The For is also ideal for use with a Fields Count and Recordset Count because there is an indexer involved and that allows for easy processing of the information. Unlike For Each, where the collection simply needs to be enumerated through, this also allows us to go to each column and row as a specifically, chosen position rather than blindly look for something in a collection.

For also works with other forms of collected data when working with XML and enumerating through a nodelist, Child Nodes, and Attribute Nodes. Since these too are also index driven.

The use of conditional Loops

There are six conditional loops

Do

Loop Until

Do

Loop While

These two conditional loops are based on the concept that one iteration of the loop must be performed before the evaluation of the condition is said to be true or false.

For example Untll(V=1) Even if V was to 1 from the beginning of the loop, it will proves the code inside that Do statement first. It also assumes the variable will be false during the processing through the loop.

Loop While, on the other hand assumes the conditional statement is true until proven otherwise.

Do Until

Loop

Do While

Loop

These two conditional loops are based on the concept that no iteration of the loop must be performed before the evaluation of the condition is said to be true or false.

For example Do Until(V=1) may already be true and would not even run if it were. It also assumes the variable will be false during the processing through the loop.

Again, the same thing happens with a Do While loop where the conditional statement is true until proven otherwise.

While

Wend

While Statements are conditional too but it is assumed that while the condition is true, it won't stop processing until the condition is false. I know this sounds the same as a normal do while loop, there is no exit while as there is with a Do while where you can use Exit Do.

Below are conditional branches. Generally speaking these can be stand alone or placed inside a loop.

If Then

End If

If Then

Else

End IF

If Then

Elseif

End If

As an example, below is one of our favorites:

Dim Pos

Pos = Instr(Object.Path_.Classname, "_")

What this does is tell me where the _ is located in a Classname. There are three possible scenarios:

1. There are no _.
2. There is one at the very beginning.
3. There is one in the middle.

If pos = 0 then

Elseif pos = 1 then

Else

End If

This is exactly the logic I needed to parse the three possible incomes from what I knew was going to happen when looking for three specific possibilities.

The use of error trapping

On Error Resume Next

If err.number <> 0 then

End If

While the use of error trapping is important, it can also mask some issues in programming that you should address otherwise, you'll wind up with a lot of if err.Number <> 0 then statements that are not only ugly looking, they defeat the real reason why you should be using this kind of logic and when.

It is strongly suggested that when you use this kind of error checking it is within the confines of a sub or function where you could place the logic into it to determine whether or not the routine determines if the information is coming in as a specific type.

I prefer to use the try catch approach:

```
Try


Catch ex As Exception


End Try
```

Suppose your program is running on another machine and that machine doesn't have the object that you want to use. If you use On Error Resume Next at the top of your program without a sub or function to test whether or not the object exists and you have a loop in it, you could find your program running in a loop where that machine uses up all its memory resources and you could be out of a job.

Instead, it is better to create a function that tests whether or not you can create the object and if you can't, then you can call a Wscript.Quit(-1).

Here's an example:

Private Function Test_If_Object_Exists(ByVal ObjectName)

```
        On Error Resume Next

        Obj = CreateObject(ObjectName)

        If err.Number <> 0 then
    Err.Clear
    Test_If_Object_Exists = "False"
  Else
    Test_If_Object_Exists = "True"
  End If
End Function
```

When this function is called:

Dim iret As Integer

iret = Test_If_Object_Exists("DAO.DBEngine.120")

If iret = "False" then

```
        Wscript.Quit(-1)
```

End If

Had you not written the code this way, and placed the On Error Resume Next inside the at the very beginning of the coding sequence, without error checking, the program would continue trying to run through the everything you told it to do and when it came to a loop, that loop would run and run and run.

Data Conversions

Contrary to popular belief, when you Dim strFirstName, and then used it like it was a string what you're really seeing in VB.NET is a Variant. To convert them:

Function	Description
Asc	Converts the first letter in a string to ANSI code
CBool	Converts an expression to a variant of subtype Boolean
CByte	Converts an expression to a variant of subtype Byte
CCur	Converts an expression to a variant of subtype Currency
CDate	Converts a valid date and time expression to the variant of subtype Date
CDbl	Converts an expression to a variant of subtype Double
Chr	Converts the specified ANSI code to a character
CInt	Converts an expression to a variant of subtype Integer
CLng	Converts an expression to a variant of subtype Long
CSng	Converts an expression to a variant of subtype Single
CStr	Converts an expression to a variant of subtype String

Hex	Returns the hexadecimal value of a specified number
Oct	Returns the octal value of a specified number

Suppose I wanted to convert a Variant to Boolean:
Dim v A Integer
Dim b As Boolean
v=0
b = Cbool(v)

Msgbox(v)
Msgbox(b)
v will return a 0 and b will return False.

Constants

Constants are static values and can be in various formats including Hex and Long.
Const wbemFlagReturnImmediately = &h10
Const wbemFlagForwardOnly = &h20
These two could just as easily be written like this:
Const wbemFlagReturnImmediately = 16
Const wbemFlagForwardOnly = 32

Declarations

I've pretty well covered this. When you Dim – short for Dimension – a variable, by default it is a Variant and I've already shown you how.

Dim strQuery As String

strQuery = "Select * from Products"

You can also use the Dim statement to initialize an Array:

Dim Names() As String

Dim Values(,) As String

ReDim Names(rs.Fields.Count)

ReDim Values(rs.Recordset Count, rs.Fields.count)

Arrays can also be created by using the ARRAY key word:

Dim ComputerNames

ComputerNames = ARRAY("Machine1", "Machine2", "Machine3")

Reg Expressions

Regular expressions -- Reg Expressions – are ways in which you can replace string values and validate strings.

Regular Expressions

String Parsing

While I borrowed this from w3schools.com simply because I would say the same thing and the same way, almost all of these are being used in my getValue function I've been using for the past 15 years

Function	Description
InStr	Returns the position of the first occurrence of one string within another. The search begins at the first character of the string
InStrRev	Returns the position of the first occurrence of one string within another. The search begins at the last character of the string
LCase	Converts a specified string to lowercase
Left	Returns a specified number of characters from the left side of a string
Len	Returns the number of characters in a string
LTrim	Removes spaces on the left side of a string

RTrim	Removes spaces on the right side of a string
Trim	Removes spaces on both the left and the right side of a string
Mid	Returns a specified number of characters from a string
Replace	Replaces a specified part of a string with another string a specified number of times
Right	Returns a specified number of characters from the right side of a string
Space	Returns a string that consists of a specified number of spaces
StrComp	Compares two strings and returns a value that represents the result of the comparison
String	Returns a string that contains a repeating character of a specified length
StrReverse	Reverses a string
UCase	Converts a specified string to uppercase

Now, look at my parsing routine:

```
Function GetValue(ByVal Name As String, ByVal obj As Object)
  Dim tempstr As String
  Dim pos as Integer
  Dim pName As String
  pName = Name
  tempstr = obj.GetObjectText_
  Name = Name + " = "
  pos = InStr(tempstr, Name)
  If pos Then
    pos = pos + Len(Name)
    tempstr = Mid(tempstr, pos, Len(tempstr))
    pos = InStr(tempstr, ";")
    tempstr = Mid(tempstr, 1, pos - 1)
    tempstr = Replace(tempstr, Chr(34), "")
    tempstr = Replace(tempstr, "{", "")
    tempstr = Replace(tempstr, "}", "")
    tempstr = Trim(tempstr)
    If obj.Properties_(pName).CIMType = 101 Then
      tempstr = Mid(tempstr, 5, 2) + "/" + _
            Mid(tempstr, 7, 2) + "/" + _
            Mid(tempstr, 1, 4) + " " + _
            Mid(tempstr, 9, 2) + ":" + _
            Mid(tempstr, 11, 2) + ":" + _
            Mid(tempstr, 11, 2) + ":" + _
            Mid(tempstr, 13, 2)
    End If
    GetValue = tempstr
  Else
    GetValue = ""
  End If
End Function
```

The ones I didn't use are: InStrRev, StrComp. strReverse, Left, LTrim, RTrim, Right, Space, LCase and UCase.

I didn't because I didn't need to search through a string from right to left: InstrRev.

I used Mid function rather than left or right

I used Trim because I wanted to Trim once what would take LTrim and RTrim to do in two separate calls.

I'm not upper casing or lower casing so LCase and UCase weren't used.

I'm not using strComp because I'm not comparing a string to another.

And Finally, I'm not adding spaces to anything, so I didn't use space.

But I am using everything else.

Working with Arrays

I love working with them, even if I am dyslexic

Okay, so here's the idea. Arrays are places where you can store information.

Dim x

Dim y

Dim Names()

Dim Values(,)

Redim Names(rs.Fields.count)

Redim Values(rs.Recordset Count, rs.Fields.count)

This is the way I can create two arrays to hold the names of my fields and the values of my fields when I'm wanting to enumerate through a Recordset set.

The routine would look like this:

y=0

Do While not rs.EOF

 For x=0 to rs.Fields.count–1

        If y = 0 then

    Names(x) = rs.Fields(x).Names

```
        Values(y, x) = rs.Fields(x).Value

Else

            Values(y, x) = rs.Fields(x).Value

End If

Call rs.MoveNext()

y=y+1

Loop
```

Option Explicit

One of the most important lines of code is this: Option Explicit. Being not one who wants someone looking over my shoulder and tells me I am not defining my variables when I know the current works perfectly fine. Never-the-less, it is good to know such a statement exists and tells me when I'm not treating this as a true professional scripting language that it is. In a new project form1 with a button, type the following:

```
Option Explicit

Private Sub Command1_Click()

        Dim x As Integer

        Dim y As Integer

        z = CreateObject("Datalinks")

End Sub
```

You will get the following error after clicking on the button:

I'm torn between tell you about this one for a variety of reasons. First, I consider it to be Option Explicit's evil twin. Two it will mask errors that you should be being told about but you won't.

Three, when you are on deadline, this can prove to be a way you save yourself from collecting unemployment.

Option Explicit
On Error Resume Next
Const x = 1000
x = 60
Error Message:

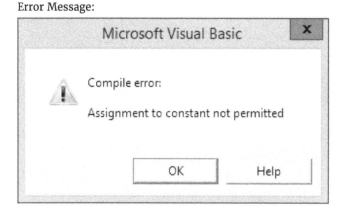

Evaluators Or ways to compare things

There are ways in which you can compare things. These, in VB are the following:
= equals
< less than

> greater than

\<\> not equal to
\<= equal to and less than

=\> equal to and greater than

Go to your Module File and create a public sub using the name of the and type this:

```
ws = CreateObject("WScript.Shell")
ws.Run("Https://www.Bing.com")
ws.Run("Https://www.Facebook.com")
ws.Run("Https://www.Google.com")
ws.Run("Https://www.Yahoo.com")
```

WScript.Shell Explained

This object is probably one of the most powerful one. Especially for us. For a wide variety of reasons.

1. The ws.CurrentDirectory is used in almost all the examples.
2. Getting a list of Special Folders will help us later
3. SendKeys can automate workflows
4. Run will be used to start Access and Excel and pull in a CSV text file
5. Popup will also be used later
6. CreateShortCut is a great way to place files on a user's desktop

That is 6 of 14 we're going to be using in this book.
With that said, let's dive into the deep end.

AppActivate

Best way to describe this one is it is a cool kind of weird.

Try this:

```
Option Explicit

Dim oAccess

Private Sub Command1_Click()



Dim ws as Object
```

```
oAccess = CreateObject("Access.Application")

oAccess.Visible = True

ws = CreateObject("WScript.Shell")

ws.AppActivate ("Microsoft Access")


End Sub
```

Access becomes the window commanding our attention. In-other-words, the method works to bring the window to the forefront.

CreateShortCut

Looks devilishly simple. ws.CreateShortcut()

Try This:

```
ws = CreateObject("WScript.Shell")

nl = ws.CreateShortcut("C:\users\Administrator\Desktop\VisualBasic.lnk")

nl.TargetPath = "C:\Program Files (x86)\Microsoft Visual Studio\VB98\VB.Net.exe"

nl.Arguments = ""

nl.Description = "Visual Basic 6"

nl.HotKey = "ALT&CTRL&F"

nl.IconLocation = "C:\Program Files (x86)\Microsoft Visual Studio\VB98\VB.Net.exe
"

nl.WindowStyle = "1"
```

nl.WorkingDirectory = "C:\Program Files (x86)\Microsoft Visual Studio\VB98"

nl.Save

nl = Nothing

My link is now on my desktop.

Works almost exactly like the Run version.

```
ws = CreateObject("WScript.Shell")

ws.exec("Calc")
```

ExpandEnvironmentSettings

Ever wanted to know what is considered a special folder?

```
ws = CreateObject(" WScript.Shell

fullpath = ws.ExpandEnvironmentStrings("%windir%\notepad.exe, 0")

ws.Popup (fullpath)
```

LogEvent

I suppose your biggest question is, why would I want to log an event? The fact is, logging an event is a great way to let others know that you were on a machine and your program launched on a certain day in time.

But there's more to it than that. This also a way you can tell technical support about an error you've encountered trying to run your script.

Eventlog severity levels are the following:

0 SUCCESS

1 ERROR

2 WARNING

4 INFORMATION

8 AUDIT_SUCCESS

16 AUDIT_FAILURE

The code to do this:

```
ws = CreateObject("WScript.Shell")

ws.LogEvent(4, "You started reading this book!")
```

Believe me when I tell you this. You'll be back!

Popup

Just another way to let your users know something has happened.

```
ws = CreateObject("WScript.Shell")

ws.Popup( "You struck gold")
```

RegDelete, RegRead, RegWrite

I am not going to show you RegDelete or RegWrite. If you want to learn how to use those two, please feel free to do it on your own.
As for RegRead:

```
key = "HKEY_CLASSES_ROOT\MDACVer.Version\CurVer\"
ws = CreateObject("WScript.Shell")
ws.RegRead(key)
```
This returned:
MDACVer.Version.6.0

Run

Works almost exactly like the exec version.

```
ws = new-object –com WScript.Shell
```

```
ws.Run("Calc")
```

Sendkeys is about the most cantankerous method that you will want to use. First, the program where you want to send the keys to has to be running and the active window. If you decide to use hot keys, the other program needs to be able to use them.

```
Dim ws as Object
ws = CreateObject("WScript.Shell")
ws.Run("Excel")
ws.Sleep(500)
ws.SendKeys("Why did you wait this long to send me?")
ws = new-object –com WScript.Shell
ws.Run("Notepad")
ws.Sleep(500)
ws.SendKeys("Wait, you forgot me!")
```

You would be surprised to know just how many people don't know the Current Directory works both ways. You can get and it as shown below:

```
Dim ws as Object
ws = CreateObject("WScript.Shell")
MsgBox(ws.CurrentDirectory)
```

Ever wonder what are special folders and how do you get to them? Neither did I ☒

The code below will reveal them to you.

```
Dim v As String

Dim ws as Object

Dim sf as Object

Dim s As Object


ws = CreateObject("WScript.Shell")

sf = ws.SpecialFolders

For each s in sf

  v= v + s & vbcrlf

Next

MsgBox(v)
```

Below is what VB.NET returns:

```
C:\Users\Public\Desktop
C:\ProgramData\Microsoft\Windows\Start Menu
C:\ProgramData\Microsoft\Windows\Start Menu\Programs
C:\ProgramData\Microsoft\Windows\Start Menu\Programs\StartUp
C:\Users\Administrator\Desktop
C:\Users\Administrator\AppData\Roaming
C:\Users\Administrator\AppData\Roaming\Microsoft\Windows\Printer Shortcuts
C:\Users\Administrator\AppData\Roaming\Microsoft\Windows\Templates
C:\Windows\Fonts
C:\Users\Administrator\AppData\Roaming\Microsoft\Windows\Network Shortcuts
C:\Users\Administrator\Desktop
C:\Users\Administrator\AppData\Roaming\Microsoft\Windows\Start Menu
C:\Users\Administrator\AppData\Roaming\Microsoft\Windows\SendTo
C:\Users\Administrator\AppData\Roaming\Microsoft\Windows\Recent
C:\Users\Administrator\AppData\Roaming\Microsoft\Windows\Start Menu\Programs\Startup
C:\Users\Administrator\Favorites
C:\Users\Administrator\Documents
C:\Users\Administrator\AppData\Roaming\Microsoft\Windows\Start Menu\Programs
```

Now that I've gone through all of what WScript.Shell object model has to offer, it is time to take your job expertise to the next level.

Since the coding for various Objects is defined and dictated by the object itself, there's little room for creativity and flexibility.

WScript Network

When you don't know what an object is capable of, how can you fully uses all of the resources VB.NET is capable of doing? Obviously, you can't. So, when I find something I think you're going to want to use, I'm going to show you things like the below table and then, I'm going to show you how to use them.

Name	MemberType	Definition
AddPrinterConnection	Method	void AddPrinterConnection (string, string, Variant, Variant, Variant)
AddWindowsPrinterConnection	Method	void AddWindowsPrinterConnection (string, string, string)
EnumNetworkDrives	Method	IWshCollection EnumNetworkDrives ()
EnumPrinterConnections	Method	IWshCollection EnumPrinterConnections ()
MapNetworkDrive	Method	MapNetworkDrive (string, string, Variant, Variant, Variant)
RemoveNetworkDrive	Method	void RemoveNetworkDrive (string, Variant, Variant)
RemovePrinterConnection	Method	void RemovePrinterConnection (string, Variant, Variant)
SetDefaultPrinter	Method	void SetDefaultPrinter (string)
ComputerName	Property	string ComputerName () {get}
Organization	Property	string Organization () {get}
Site	Property	string Site () {get}
UserDomain	Property	string UserDomain () {get}
UserName	Property	string UserName () {get}
UserProfile	Property	string UserProfile () {get}

Since I really am not interested at this moment with trying out the methods, what does work for us when I get the information by calling on each property with a {get} or a return value.

Try this:

```
Dim wn as Object
wn = CreateObject("WScript.Network")
MsgBox(wn.ComputerName)
A window will popup telling you the Computer Name.
```

Try this:

Dim wn as Object

wn = CreateObject("WScript.Network")
MsgBox(wn.Organization)

When you run this, a window will popup telling you the organization your computer belongs to.

Try This:

Dim wn as Object

```
wn = CreateObject("WScript.Network")
MsgBox(wn.Site)
```

A window will popup telling you the name of your site.

WHAT'S MY USERDOMAIN

Try This:
```
Dim wn as Object
wn = CreateObject("WScript.Network")
MsgBox(wn.UserDomain)
```

A window will popup telling you the Domain.

WHAT's MY USERNAME

Try This:

```
Dim wn as Object
```

```
wn = CreateObject("WScript.Network")
MsgBox(wn.UserName)
```

A window will popup telling you the UserName.

WHAT's MY USERProfile

Try This:

```
Dim wn as Object
```

```
wn = CreateObject("WScript.Network")
MsgBox(wn.UserProfile)
```

A window will popup telling you the UserProfile.

Working With The Scripting Object

It isn't built in but it should be. Scripting Object is a suite of tools which helps you to perform tasks that involve Drives, Folders, Files and creating and writing information out to files.

```
Name                   MemberType  Definition
----                   ----------  ----------
BuildPath              Method      string BuildPath (string, string)
CopyFile               Method      void CopyFile (string, string, bool)
CopyFolder             Method      void CopyFolder (string, string, bool)
CreateFolder           Method      IFolder CreateFolder (string)
CreateTextFile         Method      ITextStream CreateTextFile (string,
bool, bool)
DeleteFile             Method      void DeleteFile (string, bool)
DeleteFolder           Method      void DeleteFolder (string, bool)
DriveExists            Method      bool DriveExists (string)
FileExists             Method      bool FileExists (string)
FolderExists           Method      bool FolderExists (string)
GetAbsolutePathName    Method      string GetAbsolutePathName (string)
GetBaseName            Method      string GetBaseName (string)
GetDrive               Method      IDrive GetDrive (string)
GetDriveName           Method      string GetDriveName (string)
GetExtensionName       Method      string GetExtensionName (string)
GetFile                Method      IFile GetFile (string)
GetFileName            Method      string GetFileName (string)
GetFileVersion         Method      string GetFileVersion (string)
GetFolder              Method      IFolder GetFolder (string)
GetParentFolderName    Method      string GetParentFolderName (string)
```

```
GetSpecialFolder      Method      IFolder GetSpecialFolder
(SpecialFolderConst)
GetStandardStream     Method      ITextStream GetStandardStream
(StandardStreamTypes, bool)
GetTempName           Method      string GetTempName ()
MoveFile              Method      void MoveFile (string, string)
MoveFolder            Method      void MoveFolder (string, string)
OpenTextFile          Method      ITextStream OpenTextFile (string,
IOMode, bool, Tristate)
Drives                Property    IDriveCollection Drives () {get}
```

BuildPath

The Build Path Function Returns a path and name combination. Below is an example of how it is used:
Dim fso As Object
Dim bp As String
Dim Name As String

Name = "Microsoft"
fso = CreateObject("Scripting.FileSystemObject")
bp = fso.BuildPath("D:\", Name)
MsgBox (bp)

Note: This doesn't create the actual folder, it simply shows you how the path should look.

CopyFile

The CopyFile Function Copies a File from one location to another. Below is an example of how it is used:

Dim fso As Object
Dim Source As String
Dim Destination As String
Dim Iret as Integer

Source = "C:\Users\Administrator\Destkop\bMatch.bas"

```
Destination = "D:\Homeland\"
fso = CreateObject("Scripting.FileSystemObject")
Iret = fso.CopyFile(Source, Destination, 1)
```

CopyFolder

The CopyFolder Function Copies a Folder from one location to another. Below is an example of how it is used:

```
Dim Iret as Integer
Dim fso As Object
Dim Source
Dim Destination

Source = "C:\Homeland"
Destination = "D:\Users\Administrator\Desktop"
fso = CreateObject("Scripting.FileSystemObject")
Iret = fso.CopyFolder(Source, Destination, 1)
```

CreateFolder

The CreateFolder Function creates a Folder from a known path. Below is an example of how it is used:

```
Dim fso As Object
Dim Iret as Object

fso = CreateObject("Scripting.FileSystemObject")
Iret = fso.CreateFolder("C:\Users\Administrator\Desktop\HopeChest")
```

CreateTextFile

The CreateTextFile function creates a text file in a know folder. Below is how it works:

```
Dim fso As Object
Dim Iret As Integer

fso = CreateObject("Scripting.FileSystemObject")
```

Iret = fso.CreateTextFile("C:\Users\Administrator\Desktop\HopeChest\Warren.txt", 1)

DeleteFile

The CreateTextFile function creates a text file in a known folder. Below is how it works:

```
Dim fso As Object
Dim Iret As Integer

fso = CreateObject("Scripting.FileSystemObject")
Iret = fso.DeleteFile("C:\Users\Administrator\Desktop\HopeChest\Warren.txt", 1)
```

DeleteFolder

The DeleteFolder Function deletes a folder and contents from a known path. Below is an example of how it is used:

```
Dim fso As Object
Dim Iret as Integer
fso = CreateObject("Scripting.FileSystemObject")
Iret = fso.DeleteFolder("C:\Users\Administrator\Desktop\Homeland")
```

DriveExists

Used to determine if a drive exists. Below is an example of it in use:

```
Dim fso As Object
```

```
fso = CreateObject("Scripting.FileSystemObject")
```

```
If fso.DriveExists("z") Then

    MsgBox ("This drive exists")

Else

    MsgBox ("This drive does not exist")

End If
```

FileExists

Used to determine if a file exists. Below is an example of it in use:

```
Dim fso As Object


fso = CreateObject("Scripting.FileSystemObject")

If fso.FileExists("C:\Users\Administrator\Desktop\bMatch.bas") Then

    MsgBox ("This file exists")

Else

    MsgBox ("This file does not exist")

End If
```

FolderExists

Used to determine if a folder exists. Below is an example of it in use:

```
Dim fso As Object


fso = CreateObject("Scripting.FileSystemObject")
```

```
If fso.FolderExists("C:\Users\Administrator\Desktop\Homeland") Then

    MsgBox ("This folder exists")

Else

    MsgBox ("This folder does not exist")

End If
```

GetAbsolutePathName

GetAbsolutePathName is used to find out where the script is running. Below is an example of it in use:

```
Dim fso As Object
Dim bp As String

fso = CreateObject("Scripting.FileSystemObject")
bp = fso.GetAbsolutePathName("c:")
MsgBox bp
```

GetBaseName

GetBaseName is used to return just the name of the file. Below is an example of it in use:

```
Dim fso As Object
Dim bp As String

fso = CreateObject("Scripting.FileSystemObject")
bp = fso.GetBaseName("c:\Users\Administrator\Desktop\bMatch.bas")
MsgBox bp
```

GetDrive

GetDrive is used to reference a Drive and use that to enumerate folders and files on that drive. Below is an example of it in use:

```
Dim fso As Object
Dim bp As String
Dim fldr As Object

fso = CreateObject("Scripting.FileSystemObject")
bp = fso.GetDrive("c:\")
For Each fldr In bp.RootFolder.SubFolders
    Msgbox  fldr.Name
Next
```

GetDriveName

GetDriveName is used to get the name from a specified file path. Below is an example of it in use:

```
Dim fso As Object
Dim bp As String

fso = CreateObject("Scripting.FileSystemObject")
bp = fso.GetDriveName("c:\users\Administrator\Desktop\bMatch.bas")
Msgbox  bp
```

GetExtensionName

GetExtensionName is used to get the name of the extension from a specified file path. Below is an example of it in use:

```
Dim fso As Object
Dim bp As String

fso = CreateObject("Scripting.FileSystemObject")
bp = fso.GetExtensionName("c:\users\Administrator\Desktop\bMatch.bas")
Msgbox  bp
```

GetFile

GetFile is used to get a reference a file that exists and display its properties. Below is an example of it in use:

Dim fso As Object
Dim bp As String
Dim fldr As Object

fso = CreateObject("Scripting.FileSystemObject")
bp = fso.GetFile("c:\")
For Each fldr In bp.RootFolder.SubFolders
   Msgbox fldr.Name
Next

GetFileName

GetFileName function returns the name of a specified file. Below, is an example of it in use:
Dim fso As Object
Dim bp As String

fso = CreateObject("Scripting.FileSystemObject")
bp = fso.GetFileName("c:\users\Administrator\Desktop\bMatch.bas")
Msgbox bp

GetFileVersion

The GetFileVersion returns the version of a specified file. Below, is an example of it in use:

Dim fso As Object
Dim bp As String

fso = CreateObject("Scripting.FileSystemObject")
bp = fso.GetFileVersion("c:\users\Administrator\Desktop\bMatch.bas")

Msgbox bp

GetFolder is used to reference a folder and can be used to enumerate sub-folders and files in that folder. Below is an example of it in use:

```
Dim fso As Object
Dim bp As String
Dim fldr As Object

fso = CreateObject("Scripting.FileSystemObject")
bp = fso.GetFolder("c:\")
For Each fldr In bp.SubFolders
   Msgbox  fldr.Name
Next
```

The GetParentFolderName function returns the parent folder. Below is an example of is use:

```
Dim fso As Object
Dim bp As String
Dim fldr As Object

fso = CreateObject("Scripting.FileSystemObject")
bp = fso.GetParentFolderNamer("c:\Program Files")
For Each fldr In bp.SubFolders
   Msgbox  fldr.Name
Next
```

This function can tell you what the Windows, System or temporary folder name is. Below is an example of its use:

```
Dim fso As Object
Dim bp As String

fso = CreateObject("Scripting.FileSystemObject")
Windows:
bp = fso.GetSpecialFolder(0)
System:
bp = fso.GetSpecialFolder(1)
Temp:
bp = fso.GetSpecialFolder(2)
```

GetTempName is a function that returns a temporary name that can then be used as a way to create a file. Below is an example of it being used:

```
Dim fso As Object
Dim bp As String

fso = CreateObject("Scripting.FileSystemObject")
bp = fso.GetTempName()
```

The MoveFile Function moves a file from a known path to another known path. Below is an example of how it is used:

```
Dim fso As Object
Dim bp As String
Dim source As String
Dim destination As String

fso = CreateObject("Scripting.FileSystemObject")
```

```
bp = fso.MoveFile(Source, Destination, true)
```

MoveFolder

The MoveFolder Function moves a Folder from a known path to another known path. Below is an example of how it is used:

```
Dim fso As Object
Dim bp As String
Dim source As String
Dim destination As String

fso = CreateObject("Scripting.FileSystemObject")
bp = fso.MoveFolder(Source, Destination)
```

OPenTextFile

OpenTextFile is used to read, write and append a text file. Below is an example of it in use:

```
Dim fso As Object
Dim txtstream As Object

For reading:
fso = CreateObject("Scripting.FileSystemObject")
txtstream = fso.OpenTextFile("c:\Uses\Administrator\Desktop\myfile.txt", 1, false, -2)
For writing:
fso = CreateObject("Scripting.FileSystemObject")
txtstream = fso.OpenTextFile("c:\Uses\Administrator\Desktop\myfile.txt", 2, true, -2)
For appending:
fso = CreateObject("Scripting.FileSystemObject")
txtstream = fso.OpenTextFile("c:\Uses\Administrator\Desktop\myfile.txt", 8, true, -2)
```

ADO Simplified

ADO is an acronym for Active-X Data Objects. In VB.NET, you can use it to connect to both the 32-bit and 64-bit versions of Providers, Drivers and ISAMS
The reason why ADO came about in the first place was because DAO relied a lot on disk drives to do most of the work and disk drives were extremely slow.

It is also what was used to build the .Net ODBC, OLEDB, Oracle Client and SQL Client components. So, everything you do in ADO can be applied to the various .Net world as well. Therefore, if you learn ADO, the others are self-explanatory and a walk in the park.

This toolkit includes:

- ADODB.Connection
- ADODB.Command
- ADODB.Recordset Set

While I love working with SQL Server, I use it in its simplest of terms. I create a connection string cnstr and then a strQuery as my SQL query string.

Here' how these combinations have been worked with in the past:

- Connection, Command and Recordset set
- Connection and Recordset set
- Command and Recordset set
- Recordset set

Most of my experiences deal with these four conventions although I have used the ADODB.STREAM with XML and ADSI.

Below are what you will see when these are combined:

```
Dim cn as Object

Dim cmd As Object

Dim rs As Object


cn = CreateObject("Adodb.Connection")

cmd = CreateObject("Adodb.Command")
rs = CreateObject("Adodb.Recordset set")
cn.ConnectionString = cnstr
Call cn.Open()
      cmd.ActiveConnection = cn
      cmd.CommandType = 1
      cmd.CommandText = strQuery
      rs = cmd.Execute()
```

Okay so, what is this used for? This particular code example is used to produce a forward only Recordset set. It is fast. But you can't use it for adding additional rows or perform edits and updates.
If you're wanting a more robust coding scenario, you'll want to use the connection and Recordset combination or just the Recordset set.
However, the combination of all three can produce a Recordset that can be used for adding Recordset s and editing and updating columns.

```
        Dim cn as Object

  Dim cmd As Object

  Dim rs As Object


  cn = CreateObject("Adodb.Connection")

  cmd = CreateObject("Adodb.Command")
```

```
rs = CreateObject("Adodb.Recordset set")
cn.ConnectionString = cnstr
Call cn.Open()
      cmd.ActiveConnection = cn
      cmd.CommandType = 1
      cmd.CommandText = strQuery
      cmd.Execute()
      rs.ActiveConnection = cn
      rs.Cursorlocation = 3
      rs.Locktype = 3
      Call rs.Open(cmd)
For Each obj In objs
  rs.AddNew()
  For Each prop In obj.Properties_
    rs.fields(prop.Name).Value = GetValue(prop.Name, obj)
  Next
  rs.Update
```

Connection And Recordset set

```
      Dim cn as Object

Dim rs As Object


      cmd = CreateObject("Adodb.Command")
      rs = CreateObject("Adodb.Recordset set")
      cmd.ActiveConnection = cnstr
      cmd.CommandType = 1
      cmd.CommandText = strQuery
      cmd.Execute()
      rs.Cursorlocation = 3
      rs.Locktype = 3
      rs.Open(cmd)
For Each obj In objs
      rs.AddNew()
      For Each prop In obj.Properties_
    rs.fields(prop.Name).Value = GetValue(prop.Name, obj)
      Next
```

```
        rs.Update()
    Next
```

```
Dim cmd As Object

Dim rs As Object

    cmd = CreateObject("Adodb.Command")
    rs = CreateObject("Adodb.Recordset set")
    cmd.ActiveConnection = cnstr
    cmd.CommandType = 1
    cmd.CommandText = strQuery
    rs = cmd.Execute()
    Or
    Call cmd.Execute()
    rs.Cursorlocation = 3
    rs.Locktype = 3
    rs.Open(cmd)
    For Each obj In objs
        rs.AddNew()
        For Each prop In obj.Properties_
    rs.fields(prop.Name).Value = GetValue(prop.Name, obj)
        Next
        rs.Update()
    Next
```

Recordset

```
Dim rs As Object

rs = CreateObject("Adodb.Recordset set")
rs.ActiveConnection = cnstr
rs.Cursorlocation = 3
```

```
rs.Locktype = 3
rs.Source = strQuery
rs.Open()
For Each obj In objs
  rs.AddNew()
  For Each prop In obj.Properties_
    rs.fields(prop.Name).Value = GetValue(prop.Name, obj)
  Next
  rs.Update()
Next
```

Connection Strings and Query Strings

No matter how good you get at creating database related objects, no matter how much you know about making them work interactively, true is, you am not going to do a thing without a solid knowledge of connection strings and SQL Queries.

What, exactly, is a connection string?

It is a of properties vital to a connection with a specific kind of database engine in mind that are placed together as a single string.

While that sounds too simple to be almost laughable, you might want to go here.

That might make the simple serious.

Some Typical Connection Strings

Provider=Microsoft.Jet.OLEDB.3.51;

Data Source: C:\Program Files (x86)\Microsoft Visual Studio\VB98\NWind.mdb;

Provider=Microsoft.Jet.OLEDB.4.0;

Data Source: C:\Program Files (x86)\Microsoft Visual Studio\VB98\NWind.mdb;

Provider= Microsoft.ACE.OLEDB.10.0;

Data Source: C:\NWind.accdb;

Provider= Microsoft.ACE.OLEDB.12.0;

Data Source: C:\NWind.accdb;

Provider= Microsoft.ACE.OLEDB.15.0;

Data Source: C:\NWind.accdb;

Provider= Microsoft.ACE.OLEDB.16.0;

Data Source: C:\NWind.accdb;

ISAMS

Did you know you can use a wide variety of text files as databases?

It's true, In fact, if you have a table inside a webpage, using the right ISAM or ODBC Driver, you can connect to it and glean from it the table information and convert it into a different type of database format.

In plain English, it is a text file. The idea was to take a folder and call it a database and then take a file and call it a table. Similar to the way JSOM works.

One of the biggest issues – and one that brought smiles to our technical support faces – was to explain, politely to our customers that the reason why they were getting an error when they tried to create a database was the fact that the folder already existed.

Every text file you create will have some kind of delimiter. Otherwise, placing information into a text file would be just another text file and you couldn't reuse the information because there would be nothing a program – including ours – could use to separate one field from another.

These are all various files we're going to be covering, so they really don't change that much. But they are used quite often as data storage and data files.

Of course, CSV or coma delimited is just one of dozens of possibilities. And all of these are fairly easy to code. You enumerate through names and values and then add the delimiter of choice to separate the fields.

Problem is, it doesn't work. At least, not yet. It will soon. In fact, after I get done with it, you are going to become a master of Delimited files.

ISAMS USED WITH MICROSFT JET OLEDB 3.51

ISAM Engine	Is The Folder Path The Database	Is The File Name The Database	Are Tables Internal
dBase 5.0	Yes	No	No
dBase III	Yes	No	No
dBase IV	Yes	No	No
Excel 3.0	No	Yes	Yes
Excel 4.0	No	Yes	Yes
Excel 5.0	No	Yes	Yes
Excel 6.0	No	Yes	Yes

FoxPro 2.0	Yes	No	No
FoxPro 2.5	Yes	No	No
FoxPro 2.6	Yes	No	No
FoxPro 3.0	Yes	No	No
HTML Export	No	Yes	Yes
HTML Import	No	Yes	Yes
Jet 2.x	No	Yes	Yes
Lotus WK1	Yes	No	No
Lotus WK3	Yes	No	No
Lotus WK4	Yes	No	No
Paradox 3.X	Yes	No	No
Paradox 4.X	Yes	No	No
Paradox 5.X	Yes	No	No
Text	No	No	No

Provider=Microsoft.Jet.OLEDB.3.51;

Data Source: C:\ISAMS;

Extended Properties: "dBaseIII; hdr=yes;";

What this table is telling you

Database is the path.

The File Name is the database

The file itself contains tables

Suppose, for example, you wanted to open up a dBase III database. Your Data Source would be the folder location where the file resides. The Query would be based on the filename: "Select * From [myDbase.dbf]"

If you wanted to open an HTML File. Your Data Source would be the Full path to where the file resides: C:\HTML\myhtml.html.

The Query would be bases on the filename: "Select * From [Table1]"

If you wanted to open up a text file. Your Data Source would be the folder location where the file resides. The Query would be based on the filename: "Select * From [Myfile.txt]"

ISAMS USED WITH Microsoft.Jet.OLEDB.4.0;

ISAM Engine	Is The Folder Path The Database	Is The File Name The Database	Are Tables Internal
dBase 5.0	Yes	No	No
dBase III	Yes	No	No
dBase IV	Yes	No	No

Excel 3.0	No	Yes	Yes
Excel 4.0	No	Yes	Yes
Excel 5.0	No	Yes	Yes
Excel 8.0	No	Yes	Yes
HTML Export	No	Yes	Yes
HTML Import	No	Yes	Yes
Jet 2.x	No	Yes	Yes
Lotus WJ2	Yes	No	No
Lotus WJ3	Yes	No	No
Lotus WK1	Yes	No	No
Lotus WK3	Yes	No	No
Lotus WK4	Yes	No	No
Paradox 3.X	Yes	No	No
Paradox 4.X	Yes	No	No
Paradox 5.X	Yes	No	No
Text	No	No	No

DAO Simplified

When I came to work for Microsoft in 1996, the only way to communicate with any database that was currently being used with Microsoft Windows Products was Data Access Object or DAO for short.

DAO could connect to local or remote machines and was – still is – one of the most powerful and impressive means through which one could work with data.

The reason why Active-X Data Objects(ADO) was created because it used memory instead of physical drive space DAO was well known for using. Making it slower with respect to drive verses memory.

Well, today, the speed of USB hard drives and SSD Drives makes the speed differences between memory and physical drives a mute-point.

But there was also another reason why DAO was put on the back burner.

SQL Server.

It isn't hard to imagine why. DAO connecting to a remote machine where the database was located works much like SQL Server clients can connect to a remote version of SQL Server. But DAO wasn't and still isn't limited to just SQL Server.

It can connect to all different kinds of databases such as Indexed Sequential Access Method or ISAM and Open Database Connectivity (ODBC) drivers can be used as well.

While it is true that ADO can do the same, A lot of what ADO uses and, for certain, what the .Net Framework uses has been built on top of DAO and ODBC advanced programmer's interfaces (APIs). Which is why specific types of Namespaces: ADO, ODBC, OLEDB, and SQL Client exists as separate ways to connect to different database types.

A Normal Connection using DAO

It goes like this:

```
Dim Filename As String

Dim DBEngine as Object

Filename = "C:\Program Files (x86)\Microsoft Visual Studio\VB98\Nwind.mdb"

DBEngine = CreateObject("DAO.DBEngine.36")

db = DBEngine.OpenDatabase(filename)
```

A ISAM Connection using DAO

It works like this:

```
Dim Filename As String

Dim DBEngine as Object


Filename = "C:\ISAMS\Text"

DBEngine = CreateObject("DAO.DBEngine.36")

db = DBEngine.OpenDatabase(filename,,, "Text;hdr=yes;")
```

And the Query:

rs = db.OpenRecordset("Select * from [Myfile.csv]")

To create a DAO Database:

Dim DBEngine As Object

Dim Db As Object

Const dbLangGeneral = ";LANGID=0x0409;CP=1252;COUNTRY=0"

dbEngine = CreateObject("DAO.DBEngine.120")

db = dbEngine.CreateDatabase("C:\MyFirst.accdb", dbLangGeneral)

dbEngine = CreateObject("DAO.DBEngine.36")

db = dbEngine.CreateDatabase("C:\MyFirst.mdb", dbLangGeneral)

dbEngine = CreateObject("DAO.DBEngine.35")

db = dbEngine.CreateDatabase("C:\MyFirst.mdb", dbLangGeneral)

To Open the database:

Dim dbEngine As Object

Dim db As Object

dbEngine = CreateObject("DAO.DBEngine.120")

db = dbEngine.OpenDatabase("C:\MyFirst.accdb")

dbEngine = CreateObject("DAO.DBEngine.36")

db = dbEngine.OpenDatabase("C:\MyFirst.mdb")

dbEngine = CreateObject("DAO.DBEngine.35")

db = dbEngine.OpenDatabase("C:\MyFirst.mdb")

Create and populate Table:

```
Dim tbldef As Object

        tbldef = db.CreateTableDef("Process_Properties")
        For Each prop in ob.Properties_
                fld = tbldef.CreateField(Prop.Name, 12)
                fld.AllowZeroLength = true
                tbldef.Fields.Append(fld)
        Next
        db.TableDefs.Append(tbldef)
```

Open a Recordset set:

Dim rs As Object

Use this:
```
        rs = db.OpenRecordset("Select * From Processes_Properties",
Exclusive:=False)
```
Or:

```
rs = db.OpenRecordset("Processes_Properties")

objs = ob.Instances_
For each obj in objs
        Call rs.AddNew()
        For each prop in obj.Properties_
        rs.Fields(Prop.Name).Value = GetValue(Prop.Name, obj)
        Next
        Call rs.Update()
Next
```

Time to do some summary stuff

If you have gotten down to here you should be congratulating yourself for sticking with it. But this is just the beginning of your journey. We've covered a lot of moving parts so to speak. And I'm pretty sure that your wondering why this e-book stops here.

That's because as you will soon find out, another e-book is in the wings and it will be entirely based on code. That's right. All the code you ever wanted to see in on e-book.

Well, it is coming!

The question is, will you be ready for it?

Enjoy the rest of your life and welcome, once again to the world of VB.NET.

www.ingramcontent.com/pod-product-compliance
Lightning Source LLC
Chambersburg PA
CBHW070845070326
40690CB00009B/1698